SCRIBBLERS

LEAVES
ARTY Crafty

WITH SIMPLE STEP-BY-STEP INSTRUCTIONS

Mark

Published in Great Britain in MMXX by
Scribblers, an imprint of
The Salariya Book Company Ltd
25 Marlborough Place,
Brighton BN1 1UB
www.salariya.com

SALARIYA
SCRIBO BOOK HOUSE SCRIBBLERS

© The Salariya Book Company Ltd MMXX

ISBN-13: 978-1-912904-15-0

1 3 5 7 9 8 6 4 2

A CIP catalogue record for this book
is available from the British Library.

Printed and bound in China.

Printed on paper from sustainable sources.

Visit
www.salariya.com
for our online catalogue and
free fun stuff.

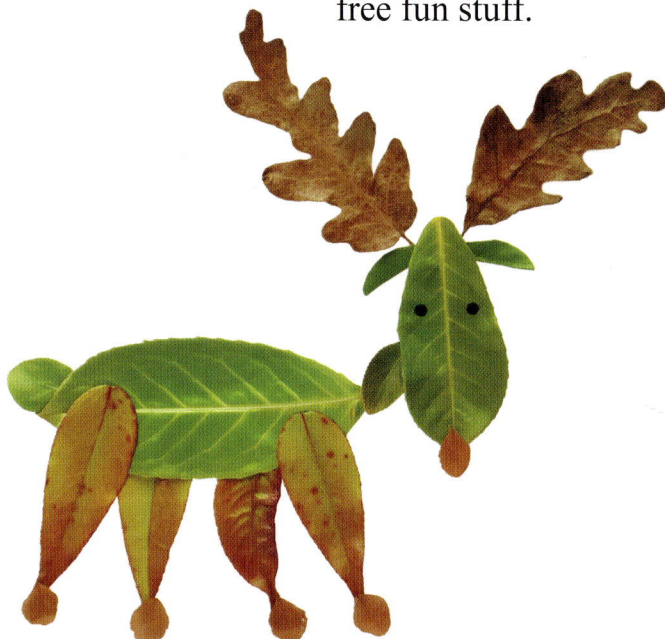

CONTENTS

WHAT YOU NEED

The crafts in this book use materials that you can find in art shops, stationers and around your home. This page shows you the materials you will need to make the ideas in this book.

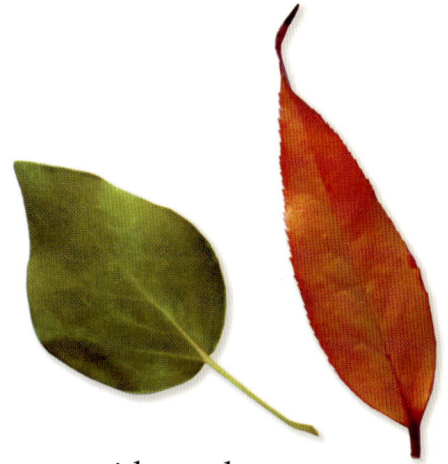

Look around when outside and you will find many different types of leaves that have fallen from trees. Collect a good range of shapes and colours.

Different seasons will have different coloured leaves too!

Follow the simple step-by-step guides to create lots of wonderful results! Find out how to make a fluttering butterfly, a thundering elephant and much more.

Mixing tray

Rocks

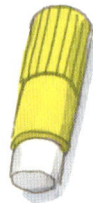

Pencil

Sponge

Pens

Glue stick

Scissors

Double sided tape

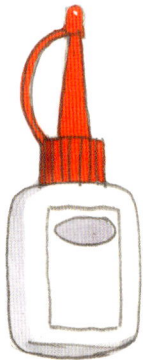

Glue

Ruler

Paint brushes

Coloured paper

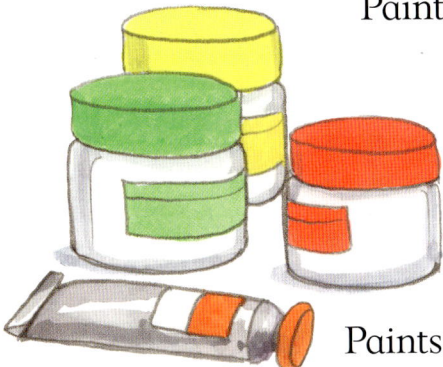

Paints

LET'S GET STARTED!

5

PERCY
the owl
Hoot!

1 Add glue to the top of a big leaf.

2 Stick two smaller leaves to the top of it, as shown.

3 Now glue two even smaller leaves inside these ones.

4 Cut out two paper circles and a beak. Glue on and add dots to the eyes.

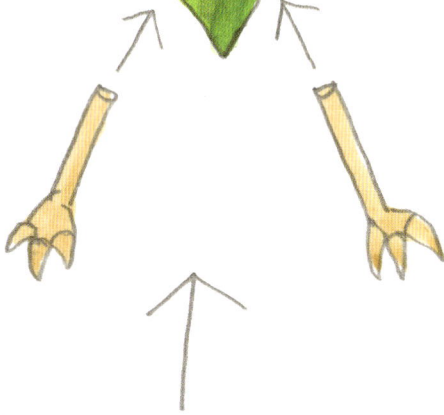

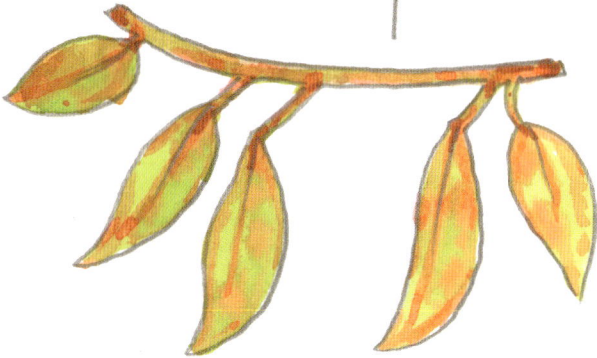

5 Glue two legs to the bottom of your owl. Then glue a twig beneath these, as if Percy is sitting on a tree branch.

Hoot! Hoot!

Hoot!

BELLA
the butterfly

Flap!

Flap!

Flap!

1 Draw a vertical line in the centre of a piece of paper.

2 Glue on two small leaves either side of the bottom of the line, as shown.

3 Now glue two bigger leaves to the top of the line.

4 Add a very small leaf at the top to make Bella the butterfly's head.

5 Glue on two twigs for the butterfly's antennae. Now draw in its face using a pen.

Flap!

Flap!

Flap!

Flap!

ANGUS
the reindeer

1 First glue down two long leaves for legs and a small round leaf for a tail.

2 Stick down a large leaf for the body (as shown). Add two more leaves for legs.

3 Glue on four small dark leaves for the hooves. Now add leaves for the neck and head.

4 Cut a small leaf in half to add ears. Glue on a small leaf for the nose.

5 Add two oak tree leaves for Angus' antlers. Use a felt tip to draw on his eyes.

Grunt!

Grunt!

Grunt!

11

LEAFY TREE

1   Cut a tree trunk shape out of a piece of paper and glue it onto your card.

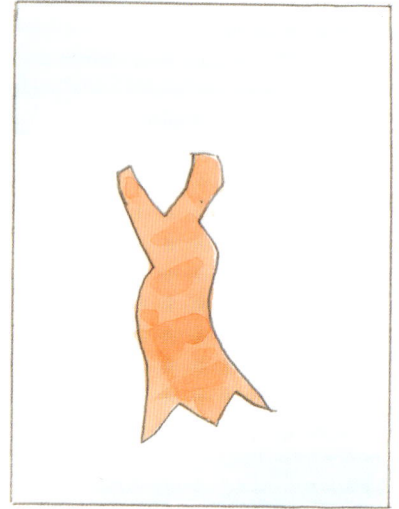

2   Add a spiral of leaves to the top of the trunk.

3   Continue the spiral, adding as many leaves as you want.

Rustle!

Rustle!

Rustle!

4 Glue some bits of grass to the base of your tree.

LEAF PAINTING

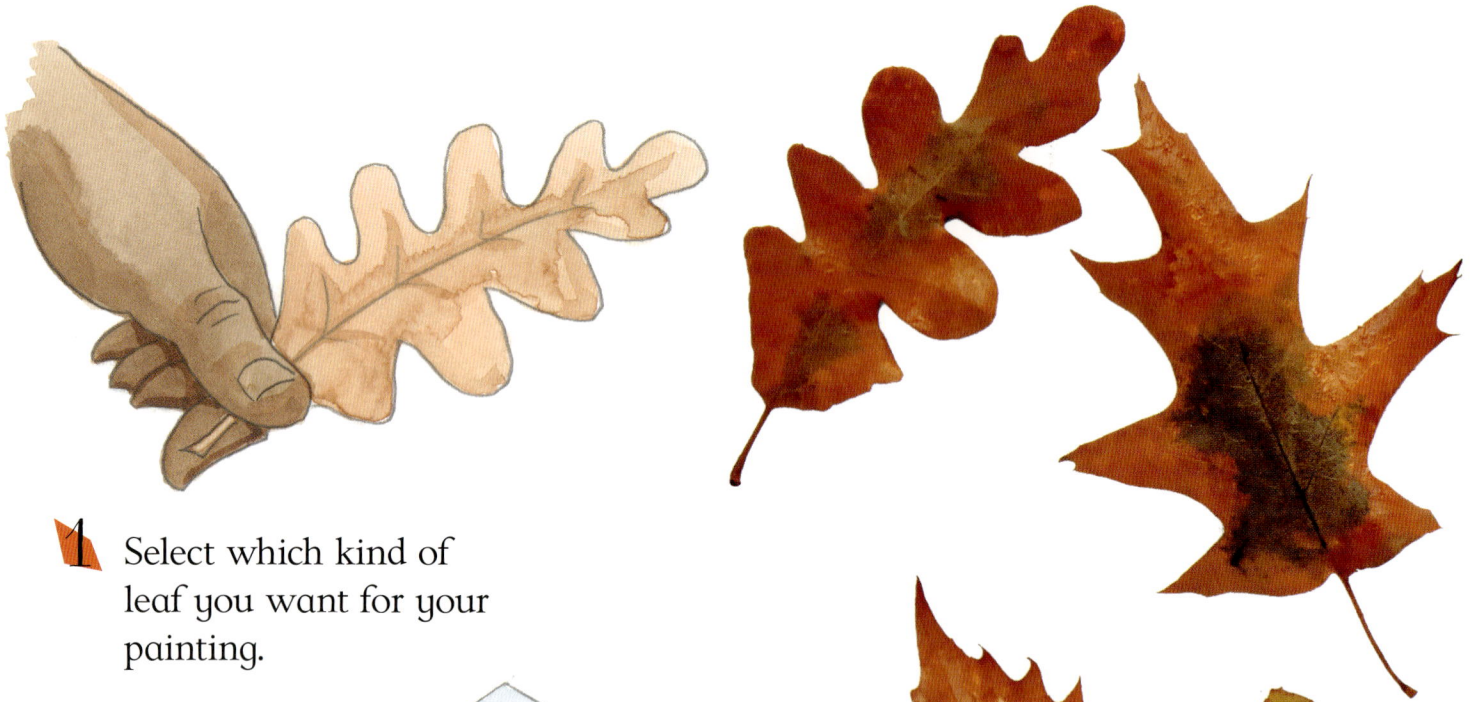

1 Select which kind of leaf you want for your painting.

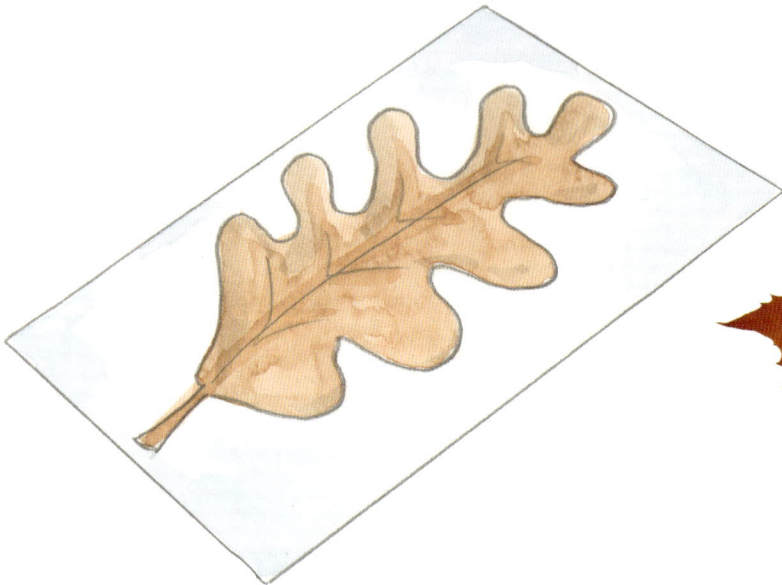

2 Place it on a piece of paper.

You will need paint, a
paint brush, a tray to mix
your paint and a sponge.

3 Using a sponge, spread
paint evenly over and
around the leaf.

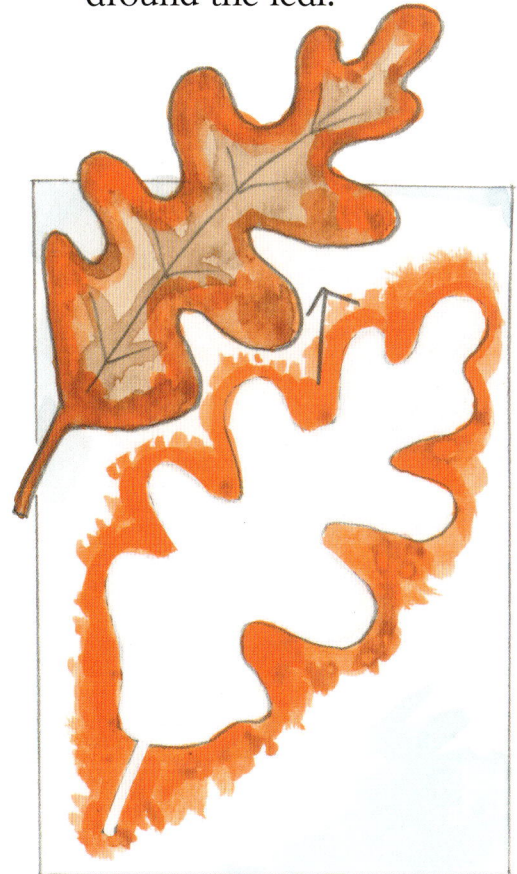

4 Carefully lift off the leaf to
see the silhouette.

HENRY AND HERBIE
the hedgehogs

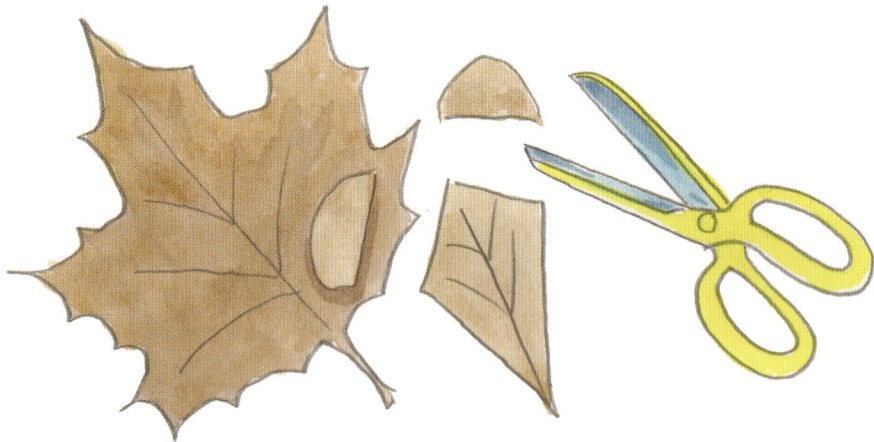

1 Cut one leaf into a kite shape for Henry's head.

2 Glue it onto a large leaf. Stick four very small leaves on too.

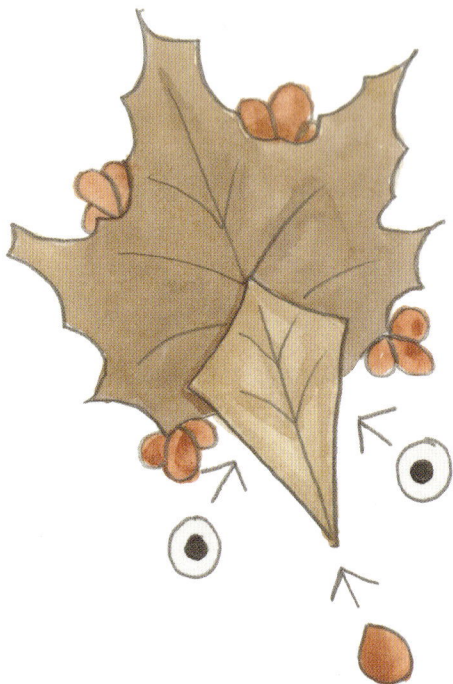

3 Make two paper eyes and a nose. Add to the head.

1 Glue together a small collection of leaves, as shown above.

2 Glue small leaves for the feet, eyes and nose to the front of the hedgehog.

Snuffle!

Snuffle!

Snuffle!

BONNIE
the bird

Tweet!

1 Cut out a circular leaf shape. Glue it to the top of a long leaf.

2 Now stick a smaller tear-shaped leaf to the body (as shown).

3 Glue three more leaves to the bottom to make its tail.

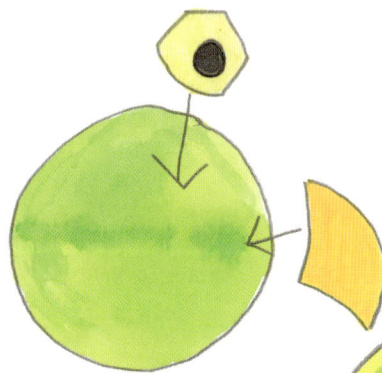

4 Glue on a paper eye and beak shape to the head.

5 Cut out two feet shapes from leaves. Glue on (as shown).

Tweet!

6 Glue on a twig (from a tree
or plant) to make a branch for
Bonnie to perch on.

Tweet!

Tweet!

19

EMMA
the elephant

Trumpet!

Trumpet!

1 Glue four tear-shaped leaves underneath a big leaf.

2 Stick on four little leaves (as shown).

3 Add two big leaves for Emma the elephant's ears.

4 Cut out her tusk and trunk shapes from leaves. Glue them on.

5 Finally, glue on two eyes made from cut paper.

LENNY
the lion

Roar!

Roar!

Roar!

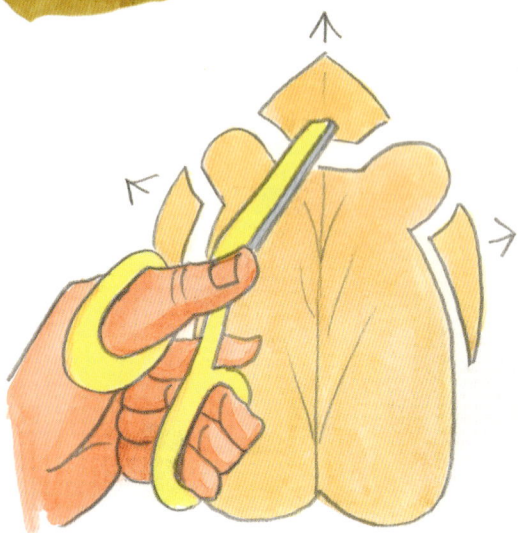

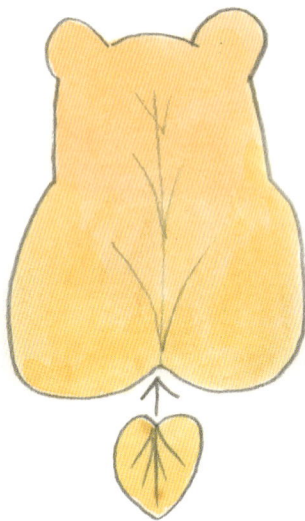

1 Cut the top of a leaf into ears, as shown.

2 Stick a very small leaf at the other end for the lion's tongue.

3 Draw in the lion's facial features using a pen.

4 Glue orange leaves onto a piece of paper (as shown).

5 Now stick Lenny the lion's face into the middle.

Roar!

Roar!

Roar!

SPOOKY ghosts

Woooooooo!

1 Round off the tip of an oak leaf.

2 Paint the leaf white.

3 Draw in the ghost's face with a black marker.

Try out these scary faces!

4 Using a piece of card, flick white paint onto blue paper.

5 Now glue your spooky ghost onto it.

6 Collect some small clover leaves.

7 Glue them to the bottom of your picture.

Woo!

Woo!

Boo!

25

DUSTY
the rabbit

1 Glue two small leaves to the bottom of a big leaf.

2 Add another two small leaves.

3 Add a leaf for the face and two long leaves for ears.

4 Cut a small leaf in half for eye shapes. Glue on (as shown).

Hop! Hop!

MARGO
the mouse

1 Add four very small leaves to a bigger leaf (as shown).

2 Make a head and ears to glue on.

paper
'go's

4 Add some plant sprigs at the bottom for grass.

Squeak!

Squeak!

Squeak!

LEAF PRINT ROCKS

1 Find some leaves and small rocks that have interesting shapes to use for this art project.

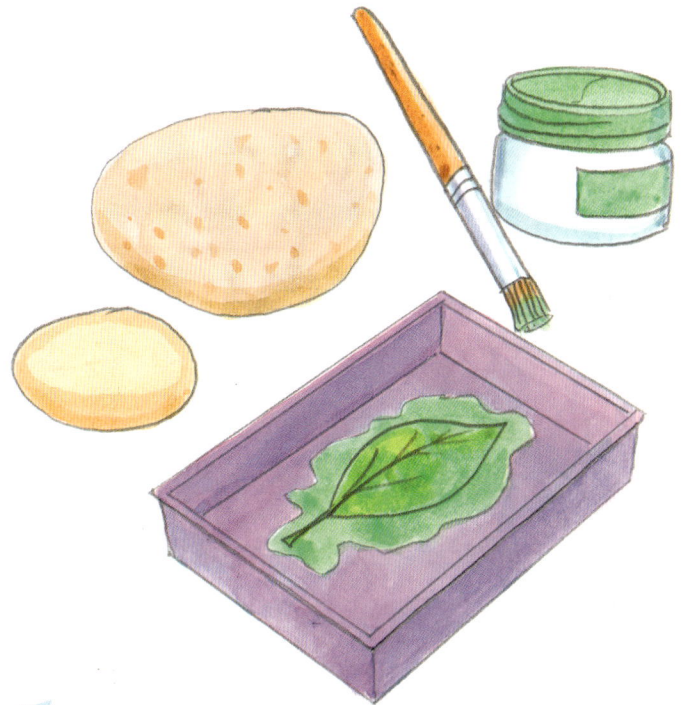

2 Paint a layer of colour over the surface of one of your leaves.

Press down

3 Quickly lift the leaf and press it onto one of your rocks.

Lift up

4 Carefully lift off the leaf to reveal the leaf shape imprinted on the rock.

FUNNY FACES

Have fun making some crazy faces by just using leaves with funny features cut out of leaf shapes.

Hi!

Ha ha!

Add odd-shaped noses, eyes and mouths.

Try using all kinds of
leaves and plants to make
crazy hairstyles.

GET CREATIVE...

SEE HOW

MANY FACES

YOU CAN MAKE!

GLOSSARY

Antennae the pair of long, thin feelers on an insect's head that it uses to sense its surroundings.

Antlers bones extending from the heads of some mammal species.

Clover a type of plant, usually with three small leaves.

Imprinted when the mark or outline of something is left on a surface.

Marker a type of felt tip pen that makes bold, wide lines.

Perch to sit or rest on something. Birds are usually said to perch on something.

Trunk the long, flexible nose of an elephant.

Tusk a long, pointed tooth, sticking out from the mouths of some animals.

INDEX